Danger Is....

By Ymkje Wideman-van der Laan
Illustrated by Jennifer Lackgren
Based on original characters by Rob Feldman

For Logan

One day I opened the front door,
And sprinted off, whatever for.
I laughed and ran right to the street,
Faster and faster moved my feet.

It scared me when the loudest sound
Rang after me, and I hit the ground.
I cupped my ears and crouched down low,
It was my grandma yelling, "NOOOOO!"

I'd never heard my
grandma shout,
Or tell me "Stop!"
in a voice that loud.

She ran to me, and
kneeling down,
She looked at me with
a big frown.

"Running off is very bad!
You could get hurt or lost," she said.
"It's very, very dangerous!"
Oh my, she looked so serious!

"Let's go inside and talk some more
About this running out the door.
When you're not careful to look out,
You'll be in danger, without doubt!"

My grandma sounded very grave.
I knew I needed to behave.
But danger, what on earth was this?
I asked her, "Grandma, danger is…?"

"Danger means you could get hurt,
Or even killed if not alert.
To stay safe and sound," she told me then,
"There are some rules. Let's start with TEN."

1. Don't touch a stove or oven that is hot.

2. Walking on wet, slippery floors you should not.

3. Always listen to grownups, stop when you're told.

4. Don't pull away when your hand they must hold.

5. Never run off in a store, or out of sight.

6. Don't pet strange dogs that just might bite.

7. Never jump, run, or play close to the street.

8. Buckle up in the car; sit straight in your seat.

9. Don't play near water, 'cause that also spells danger.

10. Never talk to or accept candy from strangers.

These are some rules I must never forget.
I might get hurt, and I'll surely regret,
That I didn't listen to what I was told,
And acted reckless and uncontrolled.

Can you remember the 10 danger rules?

I am going to listen from here on out.

I won't run to the road or wildly about.
I don't want to get hurt, or hit by a car,

Or maybe get lost by wandering far.

I'm glad that Grandma took time to explain,
The meaning of danger, and how to remain
Safe at all times by keeping each rule,
At home, when out, as well as at school.

Logan drew 10 little fire trucks and hid them in the pages of this book. Can you find them?

About the Author

Ymkje Wideman-van der Laan is a writer, editor, and proofreader. In 2006, she assumed the care of her 6-month old grandson, Logan. There were signs of autism at an early age, and the diagnosis became official in 2009. She has been his advocate, and passionate about promoting autism awareness ever since. Logan is the inspiration behind *Danger Is...?* and other children's books she wrote for him. You can find out more about her and her books at www.ymkje.com and www.autism-is.com.

Note to Parents and Caregivers

Children with autism often lack a sense of danger, and it can be difficult to teach them safety rules. My grandson was no exception. After a few near accidents, I was desperate to get through to him that running into the street, putting his hand onto a hot stove, and unbuckling his seat belt while driving, could result in serious injury.

Danger Is...? struck a chord with him, and after reading the story with him repeatedly, he started referring to it when I was cooking in the kitchen, while out in the car, or when crossing a busy road. To my delight, he stopped without prodding at the curb one day, and quoted Danger Rule #7.

I also created a *Danger Rules* key ring for him. Visually and verbally reviewing the *Danger Rules* on his key ring regularly, and especially before going out, reinforced them even more, and is helping to keep him safe.

I hope this book can contribute to keeping other children with autism safe also.

The Author

Printed in Great Britain
by Amazon